MW01248182

When She Sees the

Moon

Cherry Jones

BookLeaf
Publishing

When She Sees the Moon © 2023 Cherry Jones

All rights reserved.

Presentation by *BookLeaf Publishing*

Web: www.bookleafpub.com

E-mail: info@bookleafpub.com

ISBN: 9789357441179

First edition 2023

I dedicate this book to my Jones Tribe: DeLonte, Hunter, NaDira, Baby Jones #1, and the other Jones babies to come. You inspire me.

To Cynthia, who has shown me that being a mom, wife, and lover of God is a revolutionary act.

ACKNOWLEDGEMENT

I want to start by thanking God. For giving me the gift of writing and the passion to create art with words. I hope with being given this opportunity, it allows for people to see another side of me outside of academia. I have always been told that my lyrical writing was something to control and continue after I exercised the muscle for analytical writing. I pray I am able to do just that with the poems I challenged myself to create in 21 days.

I would like to thank my family for giving me the material for the poetry, itself. Without them, there would be no experience of my roles as a wife, mother, sister, cousin, village member, etc. I am grateful for their presence.

Breastfeeding Mama

Ounces of goodness
Blood sweat and tears got us here
Sometimes the mornings say goodnight
Sometimes the evenings say hello
Your breasts are being rented again
And again you make delicious
You make nurturing

Ounces of goodness
This labor of love has labored the love
And the award of giving life goes to you Mama
Your warrior tattoos tell your own unique story
Bag lady, I pray you keep those precious bags
The bags carry the cure
For precious life

Breastfeeding is a whole job
Breastfeeding is a whole job
Breastfeeding is a whole job
Breastfeeding is a whole job
And it's a blessing to have been employed

Hey Baby

Baby Jones frozen in time
In the womb sublime
You make mommy and daddy so proud
I'm sorry we could never say your name aloud
Hunni says "Good morning" and "Goodnight" to
you
Never knew your world would be so cold and so
blue
We removed you at the doctor's visits
Mommy's womb misses you
we never miss it
Cacti
December
Grief
These accompany your memory
I will be apart of you and you will always be
apart of me
One of my first loves
Baby Jones #1

Black Body

All of my ancestors draped
In this body
Coming out in that step
Found in the tunes
Courageously escaping
Their throats

Honey Love

I look at you
And I see God
staring back at me

You move me
To heights that aren't numbered
To depths that can't be grasped

My faith grows stronger
Because there is a you
In this world

Next lifetime
I pray we are given
permission to reunite

New-born Days

Energy fleeting
Milk dripping
Words scattered
Eyes low

Heart racing
Ears ringing
Baby screaming
Chip-painted toes

Hair unkempt
Unloaded laundry
Dishes dirty
Subtitled shows

Throat dries
Eyes water
Space collapse
The unknown

Mind sinks
Heart buries
Last minute
Go slow

Days clash
Dad Dads
Mom moms
Seeds sow

Rest

There are years
There are months
There are days
There are hours
There are dreams
Driven deep in me
That have not slept

Sister

Sister
Sistah
Sis-star
Shhhhhhhhhhsssssssta
Sis

My love
My Darling
My Gurl
Our bond is beyond tangible
Holding secrets
Between our teeth
In our arteries
In our pneumas
For our peace
For our love
With grace
With fervor

I love you dearly
Even when I call you
Out on your bullshit

Mama's Eyes

Mama reads you
Mama knows when you're lying
Mama sees you
Mam knows when you're trying

Mama tried to tell you
Mama ain't tell no lies
Mama went to look for you
Mama's love for you never dies

Mama wanna hold you
Mama wants to you to be strong
Mama always molds you
Mama can really do no wrong

Mama saw you
When you didn't see yourself
Mama heard you
When your spirit cried out for help

Mama listens to you
Mama interrupts you to speak her heart
Mama cares for you
Mama's eyes always play their part

Mama looks you in the eyes
She sees who you called to be
Mama soul and your soul are tied
She carried you in her womb all her life

Peek-A- Boo

My Dad loves
to play peek-a-boo
Cocoa
Melon

My Dad loves
to play hide-and-seek
I was the counter
He's lost and cannot be found

Ms.Carriage

Womb
Don't be a tomb, again
Please

I Needed That

I needed that cry
I released a long wail
The oceans of Heaven
Flooded my soul
Dams of doubt
Can't hold back my praise
I surrender all

Marrietta

i hate i spoke of your son
i just don't understand his games
we're both grown
doves cried
doves found no leaves
my ark of hope continues to empty
i havent seen any rainbows
i can tell his heart is still flooded

i seek your wisdom, ancestor
i pray to God that your prayers reach him
touches the hymn of his garment
he allowed his past to crucify him
flesh of my flesh
blood of my blood
i wish to be baptized in his love
once he has new eyes

Like Magic

He feels like magic
And it's so surreal
My love
He feels so real

Consent

Saying no
Is not the same as
Saying yes

Heal

Daily challenge
Overcoming past hurts
Overcoming past wounds
Dealing with your own demons
Listening to your own angels

It's not only what you do when you begin the
journey
but how you do it
Time alone
Time with another

Just like a scrape, wound, tear, broken bones,
emotional scabs
emotional wounds
emotional tears
you have to tend to the wound to prevent
infection
some are more painful than others

Black Woman

Thank a Black woman
For allowing you
to water her presence
with your tears

Anger

His past traumas
showed up
on his clenched fists today

Heart racing
Heart pounding
I held his heart, tightly today

Diapers

Saggy
Smelly

If I have to change
Another one
I will crawl into my bed
and never come back out

Time

Time is in this milk bag
Time is in this diaper
Time is in this nursing session
Time is in the car seat
Time is in the lack of sleep
Time is in the nap
Time is in the smoking session
Time is on a date
Time is on my face
Time is in my womb
Time is on my smile
Time is in her hair
Time is on her cry
Time is in bed
Time is on my lap
Time is on

I miss you, Husband

You share your heart
You love her and her
You tell me to wait
You tell me that's your daughter
You call her what you call me
"Baby" is all you sing
You ever miss me, Love?
You sure you're I'm your everything?

Daughter

She make me want to love better and more
makes me believe in God even deeper
She makes me have even more fun
She makes me take more chances
She helps make me more of me

When she smiles, the heaven open
What a beautiful gift you are
When they say "bundle of joy", they mean you
You're the gold, treasure, and the rainbow
My womb was overjoyed to hold you

Cherry has you, little lamb
From your head, shoulders, knees, and toes
You've been a blessing
Demons tremble as your feet touches the ground
Making room for God's discovery at each step
You make me proud
Through you, we're reaping
The harvest God promised us
Heaven will never be the same

Printed in the USA
CPSIA information can be obtained
at www.ICGtesting.com
LVHW021253310524
781674LV00013B/678

9 789357 441179